The Tort Bakery

Law in Pieces: Study Snippets

Anjanette G. Seymour, LL.M., LL.B. (Hons.)

This work is published as part of the 'Law in Pieces' series study snippets. It is intended as an educational aid, blending cookie recipes and doctrinal explanations, and should not be construed as a full textbook or novel. The content herein does not constitute legal advice. Readers should consult authoritative sources and law professors for comprehensive guidance.

Cover Design: Anjanette G. Seymour

ISBN: 9798995892373

Table of Contents

Introduction

Welcome to the Tort Bakery

Law in pieces is about taking the overwhelming and making it warm, human, and memorable. In this volume, we step into a kitchen where doctrine rises like dough, elements blend like ingredients, and the law becomes something you can hold, taste, and understand.

Tort law is everywhere — in the slip on a wet floor, the shove in a crowded hallway, the neighbor who cuts across your lawn, the friend who "borrows" your laptop a little too long. These rules shape how we live together, how we protect one another, and how we hold each other accountable. But they can feel abstract, technical, and cold.

So I decided to warm them up.

In this quick-study snippet of my Law in Pieces series, every tort is paired with a real cookie recipe — something you can bake, share, and enjoy. On the left page, you'll find a decadent treat. On the right, the doctrine it represents. The structure is intentional: as you measure flour, fold dough, or wait for cookies to cool, your mind is also absorbing the elements of negligence, the contours of battery, the boundaries of trespass, and the defenses that shape liability.

Each recipe is delicious. Each doctrine page is clear and exam-ready. Each hypo simple, clean, and designed to help you spot issues the way a seasoned baker spots when dough is ready. This is not just a study guide. It's a sensory experience. A way to learn the law through warmth, creativity, and joy. A way to remember doctrine not because you forced it into your mind, but because you baked it into your memory.

Welcome to the Tort Bakery.
Let's preheat the oven — and your understanding.

Part 1 – Negligence: The Foundational Dough

Chapter 1 – The Negligence Cookie

Brown Butter Chocolate Chip Cookie + The Four Elements of Negligence

Brown Butter Chocolate Chip Cookies

Ingredients:

- 1 cup of unsalted butter
- 1 cup packed brown sugar
- ½ cup granulated sugar
- 2 large eggs
- 2 tsps. vanilla extract
- 2 ½ cups of all-purpose flour
- 1 tsp. of salt
- 1 ½ cups chocolate chips

Instructions:

1. Melt the butter in a saucepan over medium heat until it turns golden and smells nutty. Let it cool for 10 minutes.
2. Whisk in the brown sugar and granulated sugar until smooth.
3. Add the eggs and vanilla, mix until glossy.
4. Fold in flour, baking soda, and salt.
5. Stir in chocolate chips.
6. Chill dough for 30 minutes.
7. Scoop onto a baking sheet and bake at 350 degrees Fahrenheit for 10-12 minutes.
8. Let cool until set — just like a negligence claim needs all four elements to "set" before it's complete.

Negligence is built on four essential elements. Leave me out, and the whole claim collapses. This cookie works the same way: butter, sugar, flour, and chips — remove any, and you don't have a cookie. You have crumbs. Just like a negligence claim without damages.

Negligence – The Four Essential Elements

Negligence is the backbone of tort law. It asks one simple question: **Did the defendant fail to act as a reasonable person, causing harm to the plaintiff?**

To answer that, courts look for four elements:

1. **Duty**

A legal obligation owed to the plaintiff. Often framed as:

- **A duty to act as a reasonable person**
- **A duty to foreseeable plaintiffs**
- **A duty arising from special relationships (doctor-patient, parent-child, etc.)**

2. **Breach**

The defendant failed to meet the standard of care. This is the "what went wrong" element.

3. **Causation**

Two parts:

- **Actual cause** ("but for" the defendant conduct, the harm wouldn't have occurred)
- **Proximate cause** (the harm was a foreseeable result of the conduct)

4. **Damages**

Actual harm is required. No harm = no negligence. Even if the defendant behaved badly.

Hypotheticals:

Hypo 1: The Distracted Shopper

Leslie pushes her grocery cart while texting. She doesn't see the puddle, slips, and crashes into Solomon, breaking his glasses.

Analysis:

- Duty? Yes — shoppers owe reasonable care.
- Breach? Texting while walking in a store and not paying attention.
- Causation? **But for** her distraction, she wouldn't have hit Solomon.
- Damages? Broken glasses. As such Negligence is satisfied.

Hypo 2: The Rushed Driver

Mark speeds through a yellow light and clips a cyclist who had the right of way.

Analysis:

- Duty? To drive safely.
- Breach? Speeding.
- Causation? **But for** his speeding he would not have clipped the cyclist.
- Damages? Yes, he injured the cyclist. As such Negligence is satisfied.

Hypo 3: The Almost Accident

A driver swerves recklessly but hits no one and causes no damages.

Analysis:

- Duty? To drive safely.

- Breach? A reasonable person would drive safely, swerving recklessly.
- Causation and Damages? Did not exists because no one was injured. The cookie collapses without the final ingredient.

Chapter 2 – Duty

Classic Shortbread Cookies + The Duty Element of Negligence

Classic Shortbread Cookies

The Duty Cookie — Simple, Foundational, Essential

Shortbread is the purest cookie: just three ingredients, perfectly balanced. Duty is the purest element of negligence: the starting point, the foundation, the quiet rule that everything else rests upon.

Ingredients:

- 1 cup of unsalted butter, softened.
- ½ cup of granulated sugar.
- 2 cups of all-purpose flour
- ½ tsp. of salt.
- Optional: coarse sugar for sprinkling.

Instructions:

1. Cream the butter and sugar until light and smooth.
2. Add flour and salt; mix until a soft dough forms.
3. Press dough into a parchment-lined 8x8 pan or roll and cut into shapes.
4. Chill 20 minutes for clean edges.
5. Bake at 325 degrees Fahrenheit for 25-30 minutes until pale golden.
6. Cool completely before slicing — duty must be established before anything else can follow.

Shortbread is the foundation of many desserts. Duty is the foundation of every negligence claim. Without duty, nothing else matters — not breach, not causation, not damages. Just like shortbread without butter isn't shortbread, negligence without duty isn't negligence.

Duty – The Legal Obligations to Act with Reasonable Care

Duty asks a simple but powerful question: **Did the defendant owe a duty to the plaintiff, a legal obligation to act with reasonable care?**

Courts use duty to determine whether the defendant was even required to be careful in the first place.

General Rule

Everyone owes a duty to act as a **reasonable person** under the circumstances.

Foreseeability

Duty is owed to **foreseeable plaintiffs** — those who could reasonably be expected to be harmed by the defendant's conduct.

In *Palsgraf v. Long Island Railroad Co., 248 N.Y. 339, 162 N.E. 99 (1928)*, the foreseeable plaintiff was defined.

Simply: A man was running to catch a train. The railroad guards try to help him on, in doing so the man's package containing fireworks falls, and explodes. The shock knocks over a scale at the end of the other end of the platform, where Mrs. Helen Palsgraf is waiting to take her daughters to the beach, the scale falls on her, she sues the railroad company.

> **Holding**: The railroad **did not owe a duty** to Mrs. Palsgraf because she was **not a foreseeable plaintiff.**

A defendant owes a duty only to people who are within the "**zone of danger**" — meaning people who could reasonably be expected to be harmed by the defendant's conduct. Mrs. Palsgraf was **too far away,** and the chain of events was unusual to be foreseeable.

A foreseeable plaintiff is someone who is close enough, or obvious enough, that a reasonable person would think, "If I am careless, that person might get hurt." As such, if a plaintiff is not foreseeable = **no duty = no negligence.**

The Palsgraf case teaches that:

- Duty is **not owed to the whole world.**
- Duty is owed only to **foreseeable plaintiffs.**
- Foreseeability is measured by the **zone of danger.**
- If the plaintiff is outside that zone = **no duty.**

Special Relationships:

Some relationships automatically create a heightened duty:

- Doctor-patient
- Parent-child
- Common carrier-passenger
- Innkeeper-guest
- Landowner-invitee
- Employer-employee

No duty situations:

Courts often find **no duty** in situations involving:

- Purely economic loss (without physical harm)
- Failure to act (no duty to rescue unless a special relationship exists; you are the cause of the danger in the first place)
- Unforeseeable plaintiff (Palsgraf case, zone of danger).

As such, there is no duty to act; no duty to rescue, unless the law gives you one. You get a duty to act/rescue either because of a special relationship, or because you are the cause of the danger.

Hypotheticals:

Hypo 1 – The Dog Walker

Mya walks her dog on a busy sidewalk. She lets the leash extend too far, and the dog darts in front of a jogger, who trips and sprains her wrist.

Analysis:

- Mya owes a duty to pedestrians to control her dog.
- The jogger is a foreseeable plaintiff.
- Result = Duty exists.

Hypo 2 – The Stranger at the Lake

A man sees a child struggling in the water at public lake. He is a strong swimmer but chooses not to help.

Analysis:

- No special relationship.
- No duty to rescue a stranger.
- Result = No duty.

Hypo 3 – The Unforeseeable Plaintiff

A store clerk negligently drops a box. It startles a customer who bumps into a shelf. A heavy can falls, rolls across the floor, and injures someone standing far outside the aisle.

Analysis:

- The injured person may be outside the foreseeable zone of danger.

Result: Duty may not extend to this plaintiff.

Let me add another example: Lena is unloading boxes from her car. One box slips and crashes to the ground. It startles her neighbor's dog, who bolts down the street. Half a block away, the dog bumps into Mr. Ortiz, who drops his groceries. A glass jar shatters and cuts his hand. Mr. Ortiz sues Lena for negligence.

The Issue: Is Mr. Ortiz a **foreseeable plaintiff,** or is he **too far removed** from Lena's conduct?

The Rule: A defendant owes a duty **only to foreseeable plaintiffs** — people within the **zone of danger** created by the defendant's conduct. If the plaintiff is outside that zone = **no duty = no negligence.**

Analysis: Lena dropping a box might foreseeable startle someone nearby. It might even cause harm to someone standing close to her car. But Mr. Ortiz was **half a block away,** harmed only after a chain of unusual events involving a startled dog. A reasonable person would not predict that dropping a box would injure someone that far away. Mr. Ortiz is an **unforeseeable plaintiff.**

Conclusion: Duty does not extend to Mr. Ortiz. Because he was outside the zone of danger, Lena owed him no duty, and the negligence claim fails.

Chapter 3 – Breach

Crispy Oatmeal Cookies + The Reasonable Person Standard

Crispy Oatmeal Cookies

The Breach Cookie — When Things Get Just a Little too Crispy

Breach is the moment where the defendant's conduct goes "too far." Crispy oatmeal cookies capture that perfectly — they're delicious, but one minute too long in the oven and they cross the line from golden to overdone.

Ingredients:

- 1 cup of unsalted butter, softened
- 1 cup of brown sugar
- ½ cup of granulated sugar
- 2 large eggs
- 2 tsps. of vanilla extract
- 1 ½ cups of all-purpose flour
- 1 tsp. baking soda
- 1 tsp. cinnamon
- ½ tsp. salt
- 3 cups of rolled oats
- Optional: 1 cup raisins or chocolate chips

Instructions:

1. Cream butter and sugar until fluffy.
2. Add eggs and vanilla; mix well
3. Stir in flour, baking soda, cinnamon, and salt.
4. Fold in oats (and raisins or chocolate chips if you are adding)
5. Scoop onto a baking sheet.
6. Bake at 350 degrees Fahrenheit for 12-14 minutes —watch closely

7. Remove when edges are crisp and centers are set.
8. If you leave them too long, they burn just like conduct that crosses the line into breach.

Breach is all about crossing a boundary — the moment when behavior becomes unreasonable. Oatmeal cookies are forgiving, but even they have a point where they go from "just right" to "too much." That's breach.

Breach – The Reasonable Person Standard

Once duty is established, the next question is: **Did the defendant fail to act as a reasonable person under the circumstances?**

This is breach.

The Reasonable Person

An objective standard. Not the defendant's personal quirks. Not their best intentions. Not their subjective beliefs.

The law asks: **What would a hypothetical reasonable person have done?**

Factors Courts Consider:

- Foreseeability of harm
- Probability of harm
- Magnitude of harm
- Burden of taking precautions
- Emergency situations
- Special knowledge or skills (professionals held to a higher standard)

Look for facts that show the defendant:

- Ignored a risk
- Failed to check something
- Rushed
- Cut corners
- Didn't follow a simple precaution.

Hypotheticals:

Hypo 1 – The Ladder Slip

A store employee climbs a tall ladder to stock shelves but doesn't secure the base. The ladder tips, injuring a customer below.

Analysis:

- A reasonable person would secure the ladder.
- Failing to do so is a breach.
- Result: Breach established.

Hypo 2 – The Careful Driver

A driver hits a pedestrian after a child suddenly darts into the street from behind a parked car. The driver was going the speed limit and paying attention.

Analysis:

- Even a reasonable person may not avoid this accident.
- No breach.
- Result: No negligence.

Hypo 3- The Wet Floor

A café employee mops the floor but forgets to put up a "Wet Floor" sign. A customer slips and sprains her ankle.

Analysis:

- Reasonable person would warn others.
- Failing to warn is a breach.
- Results: Breach.

Chapter 4 – Actual Cause

Domino Swirl Cookis + “But For” Causation

Domino Swirl Cookies

The Actual Cause Cookie — One Step Leads to the Next

The cookies look like tiny spirals — each ring leading to the next, just like the chain of events in “but for” causation. If you unwind the swirl, you see the sequence. If you break the sequence, the cookie falls apart.

Ingredients:

- 1 cup of unsalted butter, softened.
- 1 cup of granulated sugar
- 1 large egg
- 1 tsp. vanilla extract
- 2 ½ cups of all-purpose flour
- ½ tsp. baking powder
- ½ tsp. of salt
- Food coloring (any color you like)

Instructions:

1. Cream butter and sugar until fluffy.
2. Add egg and vanilla; mix well.
3. Stir in flour, baking powder, and salt until a soft dough forms.
4. Divide dough in half.
5. Tint one half with food coloring.
6. Roll each half into a rectangle between parchment sheets.
7. Stack the colored dough on top of the plain dough.
8. Roll tightly into a log to create a swirl.
9. Chill 1 hour.
10. Slice into spirals and bake at 350 degrees Fahrenheit for 8-10 minutes.

11. Each cookie shows the chain of events — remove one layer, and the swirl disappears.

Actual cause is about the sequence: “But for the defendant’s conduct, the harm would not have occurred.” These cookies literally show a sequence. Break the chain, and the cookie loses its shape — just like a negligence claim without actual cause.

Actual Cause – The "But For" Test

Actual cause (also known as cause-in-fact) asks: **Would the harm have occurred but for the defendant's conduct?**

If the answer is no — the harm would not have happened without the defendant's action — then actual cause is satisfied.

The Basic Rule

"But for the defendant's negligent act, the plaintiff would not have been injured."

Look for language like:

- "If she hadn't...."
- "If he had only...."
- "Had the defendant acted differently...."

Hypotheticals:

Hypo 1 – The Dropped Box

A store employee drops a heavy box while stocking shelves. It lands on a customer's foot, breaking a toe.

Analysis:

- But for the employee dropping the box, the injury would not have occurred.
- Result: Actual cause satisfied.

Hypo 2 – The Delayed Doctor

A doctor negligently delays diagnosing a patient's infection by two days. The patient would have suffered the same harm even with immediate treatment.

Analysis:

- The harm would have occurred anyway.
- The doctor's delay did not change the outcome.
- Result: No actual cause.

Chapter 5 – Proximate Cause

Foreseeability Orange Zest Cookies + Scope of Liability

Foreseeability Orange Zest Cookies

The Proximate Cause Cookie – Bright, Predictable, and All About What You can See Coming

Proximate cause is about **foreseeability** — the idea that some harms are predictable, and some are too remote. Orange zest cookies capture this beautifully; the flavor is bright, clear, and unmistakable. You can foresee exactly what you're going to taste.

Ingredients:

- 1 cup of unsalted butter, softened
- 1 cup of granulated sugar
- 1 large egg
- 1 tbsp. of fresh orange zest
- 1 tbsp. of fresh orange juice
- 2 ½ cups of all-purpose flour
- 1 tsp. baking powder
- ½ tsp. of salt
- Optional: coarse sugar for rolling

Instructions:

1. Cream butter and sugar until light and fluffy.
2. Add egg, orange zest, and orange juice, mix well.
3. Stir in flour, baking powder, and salt until a soft dough forms.
4. Roll dough into small balls, coat in coarse sugar if desired.
5. Bake at 350 degrees Fahrenheit for 10-12 minutes until edges are lightly golden.

6. Cool completely — the flavor develops as it rests, just like proximate cause becomes clearer as you analyze the chain of events.

Proximate cause is about what a reasonable person could **predict.** Orange zest is the same — you know exactly what flavor is coming. If the harm is foreseeable, proximate cause is satisfied. It it's wildly unexpected, the chain breaks — just like a cookie that crumbles when pushed too far.

Proximate Cause – The Foreseeability Limitation on Liability

Even if the defendant actually caused the harm, the law asks a second question: **Was the harm a foreseeable result of the defendant's conduct?**

If yes = proximate cause exists. If no = liability stops.

The Core Rule

A defendant is liable only for harms that are the **foreseeable** results of their actions.

Direct vs. Indirect Harms

- **Direct harms** are usually foreseeable.
- **Indirect harms** require analysis of whether the chain of events was too remote.

Intervening Causes

Events that occur after the defendant's act. They can be:

- **Foreseeable** = proximate Cause remains
- **Unforeseeable (superseding)** = breaks the chain of liability

Examples of superseding causes:

- Criminal acts of third parties (unless foreseeable)
- Acts of nature (unless predictable)
- Highly unusual events

The Palsgraf Principle

A defendant owes a duty only to **foreseeable plaintiffs** within the **zone of danger.**

Hypotheticals:

Hypo 1 – The Falling Sign

A store negligently hangs a sign. It falls and injuries a customer standing below.

Analysis:

- Falling objects are a foreseeable risk of improper installation.
- Results: Proximate cause satisfied.

Hypo 2 – The Chain Reaction

A driver negligently rear-ends a car. The startled driver drops a cup of hot coffee, which splashes onto a pedestrian walking nearby.

Analysis:

- Chain reaction in traffic are foreseeable.
- Spilled coffee injuries are not too remote.
- Result: Proximate cause satisfied.

Hypo 3 – The Unforeseeable Explosion

A delivery driver negligently leaves a package on a doorstep. Hours later, lightning strikes the package, causing it to explode and injure someone across the street.

Analysis:

- Lightning-strike explosions are not foreseeable.
- This is a superseding cause.
- Result: No proximate cause

Hypo 4 – The Criminal Intervenor

A hotel fails to fix a broken lock on a guest's door. A thief enters and steals valuables.

Analysis:

- Criminal acts can be foreseeable when security is compromised.
- Result: Proximate cause likely satisfied.

Chapter 6 – Damages

Soft Sugar Cookies + The Actual Harm Requirement

Soft Sugar Cookies

The Damages Cookie — Tender, Real, and Impossible to Fake

Damage is the heart of negligence. You can have duty, breach, and causation — but without **real harm** there is no claim. Soft sugar cookies capture this perfectly: They're delicate, tangible, and you know immediately if they're real or if something's missing.

Ingredients:

- 1 cup of unsalted butter, softened
- 1 ½ cups of granulated sugar
- 1 large egg
- 2 tsp. vanilla extract
- 2 ¾ cups of all-purpose flour
- 1 tsp. baking soda
- ½ tsp. baking powder
- ½ tsp. salt
- Optional: extra sugar for rolling

Instructions:

1. Cream butter and sugar until light and fluffy.
2. Add egg and vanilla; mix well.
3. Stir in flour, baking soda, baking powder, and salt until a soft dough forms.
4. Roll dough into balls: coat in sugar if desired.
5. Bake at 350 degrees Fahrenheit for 8-10 minutes —remove when the edges are just set and the centers look slightly underbaked.
6. Let cool on the sheet to finish setting — the softness is the whole point.

Damages must be **real.** Not theoretical. Not speculative. Not "almost harm." Soft sugar cookies are the same — you can't pretend they're soft. You can't fake the texture. You know immediately whether the cookie has the essential ingredient: tenderness. Just like negligence claim needs the essential ingredient: actual harm.

Damages – The Requirement of Actual, Compensable Harm

Even if the defendant owed a duty, breached it, and caused the plaintiff's injury, the plaintiff must still show **actual damages.**

No damages = no negligence

Types of Damages you would see in a Negligence claim

1. **Physical Injury**
   - Bodily harm
   - Pain and suffering
   - Medical expenses
   - Lost wages
2. **Property Damage**
   - Broken items
   - Destroyed property
   - Repair or replacement costs
3. **Economic Loss (When connected to physical harm)**
   - Lost income
   - Additional expenses
   - Reduced earning capacity
4. **Emotional Distress (When accompanied by Physical Harm)**
   - Negligent Infliction of Emotional Distress (NIED) rarely allows for emotional harm alone. But emotional distress tied to physical injury is compensable.

No nominal damages in Negligence. Unlike intentional torts, negligence requires real harm. You cannot sue for the "principal of the matter."

Look for examples like:

- "No one was hurt"
- Nothing was damaged"
- It was a close call"

- The Plaintiff was shaken but uninjured"

There is no negligence claim.

Hypotheticals:

Hypo 1 – The Near Miss

A driver runs a red light and nearly hits a pedestrian. The pedestrian jumps back, startled but is uninjured.

Analysis:

- Duty? Yes
- Breach? Yes
- Causation? Yes
- Damages? No
- Result: No negligence claim

Hypo 2 – The Broken Phone

A cyclist negligently swerves into a pedestrian, knocking the pedestrian's phone to the ground and cracking the screen.

Analysis:

- Property damage counts as actual harm.
- Result: Damages satisfied.

Hypo 3 – The Emotional Shock

A bus driver negligently brakes too hard, causing passengers to scream and panic. No one is physically injured.

Analysis:

- Emotional distress alone is not enough in negligence.
- Result: No damages.

Hypo 4 – The Sprained Wrist

A store fails to clean up a spill. A customer slips and sprains her wrist, requiring medical treatment.

Analysis:

- Physical injury + medical bills =actual damages.
- Results: Damages satisfied.

Chapter 7 – Negligent Infliction of Emotional Distress (NIED)

Soft Center Cookies + Emotional Harm Without Physical Impact

Soft Center Cookies

The NIED Cookie — The Delicate Exterior with a Vulnerable Center

NIED is about emotional harm — real, profound, but often invisible. Soft center cookies capture that perfectly:

- A firm outer shell (legal framework)
- A tender molten center (the emotional harm)

You cannot always see the harm from the outside, but it is there.

Ingredients:

- 1 cup unsalted butter, softened
- 1 cup brown sugar
- ½ cup granulated sugar
- 2 large eggs
- 2 tsp. vanilla extract
- 2 ½ cups all-purpose flour
- 1 tsp. baking soda
- ½ tsp. slat
- 1 cup chocolate chunks
- Optional: caramel squares or chocolate truffles for the "soft center"

Instructions:

- Cream butter and sugar until fluffy.
- Add eggs and vanilla; mix well.

- Stir in flour, baking soda, and salt.
- Fold in chocolate chunks.
- Wrap each scoop of dough around a caramel square or chocolate truffle.
- Bake at 350 degrees Fahrenheit for 10-12 minutes until edges are set but centers remain soft.
- Cool slightly — the center stays molten, just like emotional harm beneath the surface.

This cookie fits well because NIED is about hidden injury – emotional harm that may not show physically. Soft center cookies embodies this: a stable exterior with a vulnerable core.

Negligent Infliction of Emotional Distress (NIED)

Recovery for Emotional Harm Caused by Negligence

NIED allows plaintiffs to recover for **serious emotional distress** caused by a defendant's negligence — even without physical impact — but only under specific, limited circumstances. Different jurisdictions use different test.

1. **The Impact Rule (The Traditional Rule)**
   No recovery unless there was a physical impact
   Under the old rule:
   - Plaintiff must suffer **physical impact**
   - Emotional distress must flow from that impact

   Example: A car lightly bumps a pedestrian, who then suffers emotional trauma. Recovery allowed.

   Most Jurisdictions have moved beyond this rule.

2. **The Zone of Danger**
   Plaintiff was in immediate risk of physical harm
   Plaintiff may recover if:
   - They were in the **zone of physical danger**
   - They feared for their own safety
   - They suffered emotional distress

   Example: A car swerves and nearly hits a pedestrian. Recovery allowed even without impact.

3. **Bystander Recovery (Dillon/Thing Test)**
   Emotional harm from witnessing injury to a close relative
   Most jurisdictions allow recovery when the plaintiff:
   - Witnesses a **serious injury or death**
   - To a **close family member**
   - Suffers **serious emotional distress**

   This is a classic " bystander NIED" claim.

4. **Special Relationships/Special Duties Certain relationships create a heightened duty to avoid emotional harm**
   Examples:
   - Doctor-patient
   - Therapist-patient
   - Funeral homes
   - Mishandling of corpses
   - Erroneous death notifications

These allow recovery even without impact or zone of danger.

5. **Physical Manifestation Requirement**
   Some jurisdictions require:
   - Physical symptoms (e.g., insomnia, nausea, weight loss)
   - Objective evidence of distress.

   Other jurisdictions do not require physical manifestation.

When analyzing NIED:

1. Identify the jurisdiction's rule (impact, zone of danger, bystander, special duty).
2. Ask whether plaintiff feared for **their own safety** or witnessed harm to **another.**
3. Look for **close family relationships.**
4. Check for **physical symptoms** if required.

NIED is about **gatekeeping** – courts limit recovery to prevent unlimited liability.

Hypotheticals:

Hypo 1 – Zone of Danger

A driver nearly hits a pedestrian, who jumps back and suffers sever anxiety. Result: NIED under zone of danger.

Hypo 2 – Bystander Claim

A mother sees her child struck by a negligent driver. Result: NIED under bystander recovery.

Hypo 3- Not Close Enough

A cousin witnesses a relative's injury. Result: No NIED — not sufficiently close relationship in most jurisdictions.

Defenses

Chapter 8 – Assumption of Risk

Almond Biscotti + Voluntary Encounter of a Known Risk

Almond Biscottie

The Assumption of Risk Cookie – You know It's Crunchy Before You Bite

Assumption of risk is all about **knowing what you're getting into** and choosing to proceed anyway. Biscotti captures that perfectly: it's intentionally crunchy, intentionally firm, intentionally twice-baked. You don't bite into biscotti expecting softness — you assume the risk of that satisfying crunch.

Ingredients:

- 1/2 cup of unsalted butter, softened
- 1 cup of granulated sugar
- 2 large eggs
- 1 tsp. vanilla extract
- 1 tsp. almond extract
- 2 ½ cups all-purpose flour
- 1 ½ tsp. baking powder
- ½ tsp. salt
- 1 cup sliced almonds

Instructions:

1. Cream butter and sugar until smooth.
2. Add eggs, vanilla, and almond extract; mix well.
3. Stir in flour, baking powder, and salt until a thick dough forms.
4. Fold in sliced almonds.
5. Shape dough into two long logs on a baking sheet.

6. Bake at 350 degrees Fahrenheit for 25 minutes.
7. Cool slightly, then slice into biscotti pieces.
8. Return slices to the oven and bake 10 minutes per side until crisp.
9. These cookies are intentionally crunchy — you know exactly what you're getting into, just like assumption of risk.

Assumption of risk requires **knowledge** and **voluntary choice.** Biscotti is the same: you know it's firm, you know it's crunchy, and you choose to bite anyway. NO one can complain that biscotti is "too hard" — that's the whole point. Just like a plaintiff can't complain about a risk they knowingly embraced.

Assumption of Risk – Voluntary, Knowing Acceptance of a Specific Risk

Assumption of risk is a defense that limits or bars recovery when the plaintiff **knew of a risk** and **voluntarily chose to encounter it.**

1. **Express Assumption of Risk**
   The plaintiff **explicitly agrees** to accept the risk.
   Examples:
   -Signing a wavier
   -Clicking "I agree" on liability form
   -Verbally consenting to a known danger
   -This usually bars recovery entirely

   Note: Because a person signs a waiver does not automatically bar recovery, there are instances when certain liabilities cannot be waived. The Courts look at:
   1. Gross negligence/ recklessness, willful or wanton misconduct, intentional torts – so if the defendant's conduct is beyond ordinary negligence, it does not bar recovery.
   2. Waiver must be clear, specific, and unambiguous. If it is: vague, overly broad, not clearly relevant to the activity, then it would not bar recovery.
   3. Public policy limits – even if perfectly drafted the waiver is unenforceable if it violates public policy.

2. **Implied Assumption of Risk**
   The plaintiff **conduct** shows they accept the risk.
   Examples:
   -Attending a baseball game (risk of foul balls)
   -Walking on clearly/visibly icy steps
   -Participating in contact sports (flag football, rugby)
   -this often reduces recovery under comparative fault.

   Elements:
   -Knowledge of the risk
   -Appreciation of the risk
   -Voluntary acceptance of the risk

Note:
-The risk must be **specific,** not general.
-Hidden or unexpected dangers are not assumed.
-Minors and individuals without capacity may not be able to assume the risk.
-If the plaintiff **knew, understood,** and **chose** the risk, assumption of risk is likely in play.

Hypotheticals:

Hypo 1 – The Foul Ball

A fan sits near the field at a baseball game and is hit by a foul ball.

Analysis:

- Foul balls are well-known risk.
- Fan voluntarily attended.
- Result: Assumption of risk applies.

Hypo 2 – The Hidden Hole

A runner uses a public trail and steps into a deep, unmarked hole hidden by the leaves.

Analysis:

- The risk was not obvious or known
- Result: No assumption of risk.

Hypo 3 – The Icy Steps

A tenant sees that the apartment steps are covered in ice but chooses to walk down them anyway.

Analysis:

- Risk was visible.
- Voluntary encounter.

- Result: Assumption of risk applies.

Hypo 4 – The Waiver at the Gym

A gym member signs a waiver acknowledging the risk of injury from equipment use. Later, they injure their shoulder while lifting weights.

Analysis:

- Express assumption of risk.
- Result: Claim likely barred.

Chapter 9 - Comparative Fault (sometimes called Comparative Negligence)

Half and Half Marble Cookies + Apportioning Responsibility

Half and Half Marble Cookies

The Comparative Fault (Negligence) Cookie — When responsibility is Shared

Comparative fault is all about **sharing responsibility** — dividing blame between the plaintiff and defendant based on how much each contributed to the harm. These marble cookies embody that idea beautifully: two doughs swirled together, each contributing to the final cookie. Neither flavor dominates. Neither disappears. They coexist — just like fault in comparative negligence.

Ingredients:

- 1 cup of unsalted butter, softened
- 1 cup of granulated sugar
- 1 large egg
- 2 tsps. vanilla extract
- 2 ½ cups all-purpose flour
- 1 tsp. baking powder
- ½ tsp. salt
- 2 tbsps. Cocoa powder (for half the dough)

Instructions:

1. Cream butter and sugar until fluffy.
2. Add egg and vanilla; mix well.
3. Stir in flour, baking powder, and salt until a soft dough forms.
4. Divide dough in half.
5. Add cocoa powder to one half to create a chocolate dough.

6. Pince pieces of dough together and gently swirl to create a marbled effect.
7. Scoop onto a baking sheet.
8. Bake at 350 degrees Fahrenheit for 10-12 minutes until edges are set.
9. Cool completely — each cookie shows the swirl of shared responsibility.

Comparative fault is about **portion** — how much each party contributed to the harm. These cookies visually show that blend: part vanilla, part chocolate, neither fully responsible for the final shape. Responsibility is shared.

Comparative Fault (Negligence) – Apportioning Responsibility Between the Plaintiff and Defendant

Comparative fault reduces the plaintiff's recovery based on their own share of negligence.

Two Types of Comparative Fault (Negligence):

1. **Pure Comparative Fault:**
   Under pure comparative fault, a plaintiff can recover damages **no matter how high their percentage of fault is.** Their recovery is simply **reduced by their percentage of fault.** Even if the plaintiff is **99% at fault**, they can recover **1% damages.**

   -Plaintiff sues defendant for negligence.
   -The jury finds the **plaintiff is 80% at fault** and the **defendant is 20% at fault**.
   -**Total damages are assessed at $100,000.00.**

   The recovery for the plaintiff under pure comparative fault in this scenario is $20,000.00 because the plaintiff can only receive damages in the amount that is not their fault, as the defendant was found only to be 20% liable of the $100,000.00 it amounts to the 100,000 multiplied by 20% = $20,000.00.

2. **Modified Comparative Fault:**
   Under modified comparative fault, a plaintiff's recovery is reduced by their percentage of fault. However, if the plaintiff's fault reaches a jurisdictional threshold, recovery is barred:
   -50% Bar Rule: recovery barred if plaintiff is **50% or more at fault.**
   -51% Bar Rule: recovery barred if plaintiff is **greater than 50% at fault.**
   -Plaintiff sues defendant for negligence.
   -the jury finds the **plaintiff is 40% at fault** and the **defendant is 60% at fault.**
   -Total damages are assessed at $100,000.00.

As such the amount of the plaintiff's fault is under the threshold, therefore the plaintiff is entitled to damages in the amount of $60, 000. This is the amount that the plaintiff is not at fault, 100,000 multiplied by 60% = $60,000.00

-the jury finds the **plaintiff is 55% at fault** and the **defendant is 45% at fault.**

-Total damages are assessed at $100,000.00.

As such the plaintiff's fault is above the threshold, they are 55% at fault. In this jurisdiction the plaintiff is not allowed to recover damages, as they are more at fault for their injuries than the defendant.

Hypotheticals:

Hypo 1 – The Distracted Pedestrian

A pedestrian crosses the street while texting. A driver, going slightly over the speed limit, hits them. The jury finds:

- The pedestrian: 40% at fault
- The driver: 60% at fault

Analysis:

- Under both pure and modified comparative fault, plaintiff recovers 60% of damages.
- Result: Recovery reduced, not barred.

Hypo 2 – The 51% Bar

A cyclist swerves into traffic without looking. A driver is also speeding. The jury finds:

- The cyclist: 55% at fault
- The driver: 45% at fault

Analysis:

- In a 51% bar jurisdiction, plaintiff is more at faut than the defendant.
- Result: No recovery.

Hypo 3 – The Pure Rule

A shopper ignores the **"Wet Floor"** sign and slips. The store also failed to mop properly. The jury finds:

- The shopper: 70% at fault.
- The store: 30% at fault.

Analysis:

- In pure comparative fault, the plaintiff still recovers 30%.
- Result: Reduced recovery.

Hypo 4 – The Shared Blame

A driver runs a stop sign. Another driver is speeding. They collide. The jury finds:

- Driver A: 50% at fault.
- Driver B: 50% at fault.

Analysis:

- In 50% bar jurisdiction, plaintiff can recover.
- In 51% bar jurisdiction, plaintiff can also recover.

Let me give an example in regard to the 51% bar jurisdiction:

-Plaintiff is 50%
-Defendant is 50%
-Damages is $100,000.00

As such the plaintiff's recovery is 100,000 multiplied by 50% = $50,000.00. IF the plaintiff was 51% at fault and the defendant 49% at fault in the 51% jurisdiction barred from recovery.

Chapter 10 – Contributory Negligence

"One Mistake" Meringues + The Harsh Bar Rule

"One Mistake" Meringues

The Contributory Negligence Cookie – One Wrong Move, and It all Falls Apart

Contributory negligence is the strictest of all negligence defenses: **If the plaintiff is even 1% at fault, they recover nothing.** It's the "one mistake" rule. Meringues are the perfect metaphor. They're delicate, precise, and unforgiving. One drop of yolk, one moment of overmixing, one second too long in the oven — and the whole batch collapses.

Ingredients:

- 3 large egg whites
- ¾ cup of granulated sugar
- ¼ tsp. cream of tartar
- 1 tsp. of vanilla extract

Instructions:

1. Preheat oven to 225 degrees Fahrenheit. Line a baking sheet with parchment.
2. Beat egg whites slowly and cream of tartar until soft peaks form.
3. Slowly add sugar, one tablespoon at a time, beating until stiff, glossy peaks from.
4. Add vanilla and beat briefly to incorporate.
5. Pipe or spoon meringue onto the baking sheet.
6. Bake for 1 hour, then turn off the oven and let meringues cool inside for another hour.
7. Handle gently — one mistake can ruin the texture, just like one small mistake can bar recovery under contributory negligence.

Contributory negligence is harsh. Unforgiving. Unyielding. Just like meringues. One tiny error, and the plaintiff loses everything — just as one tiny error can cause a meringue to collapse.

Contributory Negligence — The All or Nothing Bar to Recovery

Contributory negligence is one of the oldest and strictest negligence defenses. It exists in only a handful of jurisdictions today, but it is still heavily tested because of its dramatic consequences.

The Rule

If the plaintiff is **even slightly negligent,** they are **completely barred** from recovery.

Elements

- Plaintiff failed to exercise reasonable care for their own safety
- Plaintiff's negligence contributed to their injury
- Any degree of fault, no matter how small, bars recovery

Side Bar:

- This doctrine is extremely harsh and widely criticized.
- Most states have replaced it with comparative fault
- A few jurisdictions still use it (e.g. Alabama, Maryland, North Carolina, Virginia and D.C.).
- The "last clear chance" doctrine can sometimes save the plaintiff.

Last Clear Chance Doctrine

- If the defendant had the **final opportunity** to avoid the harm and failed to do so, the plaintiff may still recover despite contributory negligence.

Hypotheticals:

Hypo 1 – The Distracted Walker

A pedestrian crosses the street while looking at their phone. A speeding driver hits them. The pedestrian is found 5% at fault.

Analysis:

- In a contributory negligence jurisdiction, any fault bars recovery.
- Result: Plaintiff recovers nothing.

Hypo 2 – The Last Clear Chance

A cyclist negligently swerves into the road. A driver sees them in time to brake but chooses to accelerate instead.
Analysis:

- Cyclist negligent = normally barred
- Driver had the last clear chance to avoid harm.
- Result: Cyclist may still recover.

Hypo 3 – The Slippery Floor

A shopper ignores a "Wet Floor" sign and slips. The store also failed to clean properly.

Analysis:

- Shopper negligent, even slightly.
- Result: Claim barred in contributory negligence jurisdictions.

Hypo 4 – The Careless Passenger

A passenger rides without a seatbelt. A negligent driver hits the car.

Analysis:

- Passenger failure to wear a seatbelt contributed to their injury.
- Result: Recovery barred.

Part 2 – Intentional Torts

Intentional torts are part of the tort law where the defendant's actions aren't careless — they're **purposeful.** These are the wrongs that happen when someone means to do the act that causes the harm, even if they didn't mean the exact injury that followed. Think of them as "deliberate" side of civil wrongs: acts done with intent, choice, or certainty that contact or interference will occur.

Chapter 11 – Battery

Molten Chocolate Lava Cookies + Harmful of Offensive Contact

Molten Chocolate Lava Cookies

The Battery Cookie – Direct, Hot, Immediate Contact

Battery is all about **contact** — intentional, immediate, and unmistakable. These molten lava cookies capture that feeling perfectly: crisp on the outside, molten in the center, delivering a burst of heat and impact the moment you bite into them.

Ingredients:

- Bodily harm
- ½ cup of unsalted butter
- 1 cup of semisweet chocolate chips
- 1 cup of powdered sugar
- 2 large eggs
- 1 tsp. of vanilla extract
- 1 cup of all-purpose flour
- ¼ tsp. of salt

Instructions:

1. Melt butter and chocolate together in a saucepan or microwave until smooth.
2. Wisk in powdered sugar until glossy.
3. Add eggs and vanilla; mix until thick and shiny.
4. Fold in flour and salt.
5. Chill dough for 20 minutes, this helps to keep the centers molten.
6. Scoop generous tablespoons onto a baking sheet.
7. Bake at 375 degrees Fahrenheit for 8-9 minutes, edges should be set, centers soft.

8. Serve warm so the molten center flows—just like the "hot" contact as the heart of battery.

Battery requires contact, something that touches the plaintiff's body or something closely connected to it. These cookies are all about the moment of contact: crisp shell, molten center, immediate impact. You feel it instantly. So does the plaintiff in a battery case.

Battery – Intentional, Harmful or Offensive Contact

Battery protects a person's right to bodily integrity. It doesn't matter if the defendant meant to cause harm, it is only concerned that the **contact is made.**

Elements of Battery:

- **Intent**
  -Purpose to cause contact, or
  -Knowledge with substantial certainty that contact will occur

- **Act**
  -A volitional movement (volitional – done by choice, will or conscious decision rather than by accident.)

- **Contact**
  -Harmful or offensive
  -Direct or indirect (objects count) E.g. Mary pulls Tina's handbag.

- **Causation**
  -The act must cause the contact

Note: The contact does not have to cause injury. Offensive contact is enough — a contact that would offend a **reasonable sense of dignity.** Contact with objects "closely associated" with the body counts (e.g., a purse, a plate, a cane, cell phone). Battery does not require awareness —a person can be asleep or unconscious (e.g., running your hand over a sleeping person's cheeks or a dentist pulling a tooth the patient did not consent to be pulled).

If a defendant meant to touch the plaintiff (or an object they're holding or on their body/person), it is almost always battery.

Hypotheticals:

Hypo 1 – The Flicked Frosting

Jordan flicks a spoonful of frosting at Maya during a party. It lands on her cheek.

Analysis:

- Intent to throw frosting = intent to cause contact.
- Contact occurred.
- Offensive contact is enough.
- Result: Battery

Hypo 2 – The Pulled Chair

A student pulls a chair out from under another student as a prank. The student falls and is injured.

Analysis:

- Intent to move the chair = intent to cause contact with the floor.
- Harmful contact occurred.
- Result: Battery

Hypo 3 – The Grabbed Backpack

A man grabs a woman's backpack to stop her from leaving.

Analysis:

- Contact with the object closely associated with her body counts.
- Offensive contact.
- Result: Battery.

Hypo 4 – The Unseen Touch

A nurse intentionally touches a patient's arm without consent while the patient is asleep.

Analysis:

- Awareness is not required.
- Intentional contact occurred.
- Result: Battery.

Chapter 12 – Assault

Crackling Sugar Cookies + Apprehension of Imminent Contact

Crackling Sugar Cookies

The Assault Cookie — A Spark, A Crackle, A Moment of Apprehension

Assault is about **anticipation** — the moment before contact, the spark of fear or apprehension that something is about to happen. Crackling sugar cookies embody that moment: crisp edges, crackled tops, a texture that looks like something is about to break open.

Ingredients:

- 1 cup of unsalted butter, softened
- 1 ½ cups of granulated sugar
- 1 large egg
- 1 tsp. of vanilla extract
- 2 ¾ cups of all-purpose flour
- 1 tsp. baking soda
- ½ tsp. baking powder
- ½ tsp. of salt
- Extra sugar for rolling

Instructions:

1. Cream butter and sugar until light and fluffy
2. Add egg and vanilla extract; mix well
3. Stir in flour, baking soda, baking powder, and salt until a soft dough forms.
4. Roll dough into balls and coat in sugar.
5. Bake at 350 degrees Fahrenheit for 10-12 minutes until the tops crackle.

6. Cool on the sheet — the crackle deepens as they rest, just like apprehension builds before contact.

Assault is about the **crackling moment before contact** — the fear, the anticipation, the imminent threat. These cookies visually capture that tension: the surface breaks, the lines spread, and the cookie looks like it's about to burst. That's assault: the moment before the impact.

Assault – Intent + Reasonable Apprehension of Imminent Harmful or Offensive Contact

Assault protects a person's right to feel safe from unwanted contact. It is not about the contact itself — it's about the **threat of imminent contact.**

Elements of Assault:

- **Intent**
  -Purpose to cause apprehension, **or**
  -Knowledge with substantial certainty that apprehension will occur

- **Act**
  -A volitional movement creating the apprehension of imminent contact.

- **Reasonable Apprehension**
  -Plaintiff must believe contact is about to occur
  -Fear is not required – only awareness

- **Imminence**
  -No significant delay

- **Causation**

The plaintiff must be aware of the threat at the time. If the plaintiff sees the act and reasonably believes contact is about to happen, assault is almost always satisfied.

Hypotheticals:

Hypo 1 – The Raised Rolling Pin

Tara raises a rolling pin and swings it toward Tia, stopping inches from his face.

Analysis:

- Intent to create apprehension
- Tia sees the swing
- Contact appears imminent.
- Result: Assault

Hypo 2 – The Empty Threat

A man yells, "I'm going to punch you!" from across a parking lot but makes no movement toward the person.

Analysis:

- Words alone, no imminent ability
- Result: No assault

Hypo 3 – The Hidden Knife

A person sneaks up behind someone with a knife but never makes their presence known.

Analysis:

- Plaintiff unaware = no apprehension
- Result: No assault

Hypo 3 – The Thrown Cup

A woman angrily throws a cup at her coworker. He sees it flying towards him and ducks. It misses.

Analysis:

- Intent to cause apprehension.
- Appearance of imminent contact
- Actual contact not required
- Result: Assault

Chapter 13 – False Imprisonment

Jam Filled Thumbprint Cookies + Confinement Without Escape

Jam Filled Thumbprint Cookies

The False Imprisonment Cookie — A Soft Exterior with a Confined Center

False imprisonment is about **confinement** — restricting someone's movement within boundaries they cannot reasonably escape. Thumbprint cookies embody this beautifully: a soft, buttery exterior surrounding a center of jam that stays exactly where it's placed. The jam is confined. Contained. Held in place.

Ingredients:

- 1 cup of unsalted butter, softened
- 2/3 cups of granulated sugar
- 2 large egg yolks
- 1 tsp. vanilla extract
- 2 cups all-purpose flour
- ½ tsp. of salt
- ½ cup jam (raspberry, strawberry, or apricot works beautifully)

Instructions:

1. Cream butter and sugar until smooth and pale.
2. Add egg yolks, and vanilla, mix well until combined.
3. Stir in flour and salt until a soft dough forms.
4. Roll dough into 1 inch balls.
5. Press your thumb into the center of each ball to create a 'confinement space.'

6. Fill each indentation with a small spoonful of jam.
7. Bake at 350 degrees Fahrenheit for 12-14 minutes until edges are lightly golden.
8. Cool completely — the jam stays confined in its little space, just like a plaintiff in false imprisonment.

False imprisonment is about boundaries — physical or implied — that restrict a person's freedom of movement. The jam in the thumbprint cookie is literally placed into a confined space and held there. It cannot leave unless acted upon by an outside force. That's confinement. That's false imprisonment.

False Imprisonment – Intentional Confinement without Consent or Reasonable Escape

False imprisonment protects a person's right to move freely.

Elements of False Imprisonment:

- **Intent**
  -Purpose to confine **or**
  -Knowledge with substantial certainty that confinement will occur

- **Confinement**
  -Physical barriers
  -Threats of force
  -Assertion of legal authority
  -Duress

- **No Reasonable Means of Escape**
  -Escape must be safe and known to the plaintiff

- **Awareness of Confinement**
  -Plaintiff must know they are confined **or** suffer actual harm

Note:
-Confinement can be a locked door, blocked exit, or even a threat ("If you leave, I'll call the police.")
-Time of confinement can be brief — even seconds

Hypotheticals:

Hypo 1 – The Blocked Door

A young man sees a young lady walking by, he grabs her and holds her in a tight embrace, saying, "If you kiss me, I will let you go."

Analysis:

- Intent to confine
- Physical barrier (a tight embrace)
- No reasonable escape
- Result: False imprisonment

Hypo 2 – The Locked Classroom

A man is on the rooftop of a house, fixing the shingles. The owner of the home removes the ladder from near the home in which the man used to climb to the rooftop. The owner then shouts up to him, "reduce the cost and I will return the ladder."

Analysis:

- Intent to confine
- Physical barrier (removal of the ladder)
- No reasonable escape
- Result: False imprisonment

Hypo 3 – The Threatened Teen

A teenager tells another, "If you leave this room, I'll beat you up." And blocks the doorway with his body.

Analysis:

- Threat + physical presence
- No safe escape
- Result: False imprisonment

Hypo 4 – The Librarian

A librarian at the end of the day checked the hallway and basement, not seeing anyone, turns off the lights and locks the library before leaving for the day. Mary-Beth was in the bathroom, when she came out the library was in darkness and the doors were locked.

Analysis:

- No intent to confine – the analysis can stop here; the librarian did not intend to confine Mary-Beth to the library. It was an unforeseen circumstance that she was in the bathroom at the time of closure and the librarian was unaware of her being there.
- Result: No false imprisonment

Hypo 5 – The Open Window

A person is locked in a room, but there is a large, safe, open window they know they can climb through.

Analysis:

- Reasonable means of escape exists.
- Result: No false imprisonment

Chapter 14 – Trespass to Land

Lemon Crinkle Cookies + Intentional Entry Onto Another's Land

Lemon Crinkle Cookies

The Trespass Cookie – Bright, Bold, and All About Crossing Boundaries

Trespass to land is about **crossing the line** — stepping onto land that isn't yours, even if just for a moment. Lemon crinkle cookies embody that idea: as they bake, the dough expands and breaths through the powdered sugar coating, creating bright cracks that cross boundaries on the cookie's surface.

Ingredients:

- ½ of cup of unsalted butter; softened
- 1 cup of granulated sugar
- 1 tbsp. of lemon zest
- 1 tbsp. of fresh lemon juice
- 1 ½ cups of all-purposed flour
- ½ tsp. baking powder
- ¼ tsp. baking soda
- ¼ tsp. salt
- Powdered sugar for rolling

Instructions:

1. Cream butter and sugar until light and fluffy.
2. Add egg, lemon zest, and lemon juice mix well.
3. Stir in flour, baking powder, baking soda, and salt until a soft dough forms.
4. Chill dough for 20 minutes.
5. Roll dough into balls, then coat generously in powdered sugar.

6. Bake at 350 degrees Fahrenheit for 10-12 minutes until the tops crack open.
7. Cool completely – the cracks reveal where the dough has crossed its boundaries, just like a trespasser stepping over a property line.

Trespass to land is about **breaking boundaries**, even slightly. Lemon crinkle cookies visually show that moment: the dough expands, cracks, and crosses the powdered sugar “border.” That’s trespass — intentional entry, even without harm.

Trespass to Land – Intentional Entry Onto the Land of Another

Trespass protects a landowner's right to exclusive possession. It is one of the simplest intentional torts — and one of the easiest to prove.

Elements of Trespass to Land:

- **Intent**
  -Intent to enter the land

- **Physical Entry**
  -By the defendant
  -By an object the defendant sent in motion (e.g., throwing a ball in your neighbor's yard.)

Note:

- No harm is required — **entry alone** is enough.
- Mistake is **not** a defense ("I thought I was still in my yard.")
- Throwing or placing objects on someone's land counts.
- Remaining on the land after permission is revoked is also trespass.

Hypotheticals:

Hypo 1 – The Shortcut

Ben cuts across Diana's yard to save time walking home from school.

Analysis:

- Intent to walk across the yard = intent to enter
- The yard/land belongs to Diana not to Ben
- No harm required to the land
- Result: Trespass

Hypo 2 – The Drone Drop

A teenager flies a drone over a neighbor's yard and drops a water balloon in the neighbor's yard.

Analysis:

- Object entering the land counts as physical entry.
- Result: Trespass

Hypo 3 – The Mistaken Boundary

A gardener accidentally plants flowers two feet over the property line, believing the land belongs to his client.

Analysis:

- Mistake is no defense
- Intent to plant the flowers = intent to enter.
- Result: Trespass

Hypo 4 – The Guest Who Won't Leave

A guest is asked to leave a house but refuses.

Analysis:

- Remaining on land after consent is revoked = trespass
- Result: Trespass

Chapter 15 – Trespass to Chattels

Peanut Butter "Borrowed Spoon" Cookies + Minor interference with Personal Property

Peanut Butter "Borrowed Spoon" Cookies

The Chattels Cookie — Small, Simple, and Just a Little Interfering

Trespass to chattels is the tort of minor interference — not enough to destroy or take over property, but enough to cause inconvenience or temporary loss of use. These peanut butter cookies are the perfect metaphor: they're famously made with just one spoon, and the recipe is so simple that even a small interruption — borrowing the spoon, using it briefly, handing it back — mirrors the tort's light touch.

Ingredients:

- 1 cup of creamy peanut butter
- 1 cup of granulated sugar
- 1 large egg
- 1 tsp. vanilla extract

Instructions:

1. Mix peanut butter, sugar, egg, and vanilla in a bowl until smooth.
2. Scoop dough using a single spoon or small scoop.
3. Place on a baking sheet and press lightly with a fork to create the classic crisscross pattern.
4. Bake at 350 degrees Fahrenheit for 8-10 minutes until edges are set.
5. Cool completely — these cookies are delicate when warm, just like chattels can be sensitive to even small interferences.

Trespass to chattels is about small disruptions — borrowing, touching, using, or interfering with someone's property in a way that causes minor harm or inconvenience. These cookies are simple, quick, and require minimal tools — perfect metaphor for a tort that involves light temporary interference, not destruction or domination.

Trespass to Chattels – Intentional, Minor Interference with Personal Property

Trespass to chattels protects a person's right to the use and enjoyment of their personal property. It is the "little sibling" of conversion — less serious, less damaging, and easier to fix.

Elements of Trespass to Chattels:

- **Intent**
  -Purpose to interfere, **or**
  -Knowledge with substantial certainty that interference will occur

- **Interference with Personal Property**
  -Using, touching, damaging, or depriving the owner of use

- **Harm or Substantial loss of Use**
  -Actual harm to the chattel, **or**
  -Significant interference with the owner's ability to use it

Note:

- No need for total deprivation — that's conversion.
- Brief interference counts if it causes inconvenience or temporary loss of use.
- Mistake is not a defense ("I thought it was mine.")
- Electronic interference (e.g., spam, unauthorized access) can qualify.
- If property is **borrowed, used, moved, or slightly damaged**, think **trespass to chattels.** If it is **taken, destroyed, or kept,** think **conversion.**

Hypotheticals:

Hypo 1 – The Borrowed Phone

Ria needs to make a call her cell phone is dead, so she grabs her roommate Tia's without permission and makes her call, then places it back on Tia's desk.

Analysis:

- Intentional interference
- Temporary deprivation of use
- No destruction
- Result: Trespass chattels

Hypo 2 – The Scratched Sunglasses

Phillip sees Mike's sunglasses on the desk and wants to try them on without permission and accidentally scratches the lens.

Analysis:

- Unauthorized use + minor damage
- Result: Trespass to chattels

Hypo 3 – The Moved Laptop

A student moves another student's laptop across the room as a prank. The owner spends 10 minutes searching for it.

Analysis:

- Interference causing temporary loss of use.
- Result: Trespass to chattels

Chapter 16 – Conversion

Giant Bakery Style Cookies + Serious Interference with Personal Property

Giant Bakery Style Cookies

The Conversion Cookie — So Big It Takes Over Everything

Conversion is the tort of **serious interference** — when someone exercises such control over another's property that the law treats it as if they bought it outright. These giant bakery style cookies embody that idea: they're oversized, dominating the baking sheet, taking up more space than any cookie reasonably should. They don't just sit there — they take over.

Ingredients:

- 1 cup unsalted butter, softened
- 1 cup packed brown sugar
- ½ cup granulated sugar
- 2 large eggs
- 2 tsps. vanilla extract
- 3 cups of all-purpose flour
- 1 tsp. baking soda
- 1 tsp. salt
- 2 cups chocolate chunks

Instructions:

1. Cream butter and sugar until fluffy.
2. Add eggs and vanilla; mix well.
3. Stir in flour, baking soda, and salt until a thick dough forms.
4. Fold in chocolate chunks.
5. Scoop large ¼-1/3 cup mounds of dough onto a baking sheet — these cookies should be huge.

6. Bake at 375 degrees Fahrenheit for 12-14 minutes until edges are golden and center are set.
7. Cool completely — these cookies dominate the tray, just like conversion dominates the plaintiff's possessory rights.

Conversion is about **taking over** someone's property — using it, keeping it, or destroying it in a way that seriously interferes with the owner's rights. These cookies are oversized, bold, and impossible to ignore. They don't share space. They don't leave room for others. They represent the tort perfectly: when interference becomes so substantial that the law says, "You break it, you buy it."

Conversion – Serious Interference with Personal Property Requiring Full Value Damages

Conversion is the intentional tort that protects a person's right to **exclusive control** over their personal property. It is the "big sibling" of trespass to chattels —more serious, more damaging, and more costly.

Elements of Conversion:

- **Intent**
  -Purpose to exercise control, **or**
  -Knowledge with substantial certainty that control will occur

- **Serious Interference**
  -The defendant's conduct must be so substantial that it justifies requiring them to pay the **full value** of the property.

- **Dominion or Control**
  -Taking, keeping, destroying, selling, or significantly altering the property

- **Damages**

Note:

- Mistake is not a defense ("I thought it was mine.")
- The remedy is **full market value** of the item — not repair costs.
- Conversion can occur even if the defendant intends to return the item later. (Because the tort is complete, at the moment of the unauthorized taking or using of the plaintiff's property when the defendant takes full control or dominion, you may think it seems like 'trespass to chattel' but it is not, this is not temporary, this is treating an item as if it is your own – e.g., Jerry takes Tom's car to go Christmas shopping without Tom's permission. Jerry is treating Tom's car as if it is his own without asking for permission first, depriving

him of possession and control at that time. In a trespass to chattel situation, Jerry in a hurry for class, borrows Tom's shirt without permission and returns it after class – this interference is minor as compared to taking full possession of Tom's car as if it were his own.
- Destroying or significantly altering property is classic conversion.

Let me go deeper with my third point, I hope it gives even more clarity. **Conversion can occur even if the defendant intends to return the item later.**

1. Trespass to Chattels = Interference
The defendant interferes with the plaintiff's property, but the interference is:
- **temporary**
- **minor**
- **not destructive**
- **not inconsistent with the owner's rights in a serious way**

Jerry taking the shirt is interference, yes — but:
- Tom gets it back quickly
- The shirt isn't harmed
- Jerry's use doesn't meaningfully deprive Tom of ownership
- Jerry isn't acting like the shirt is *his* in a way that destroys Tom's rights.

So even though Jerry "controls" the shirt for a moment, the law says: **This is not serious enough to count as dominion.**

2. Conversion = Serious Dominion
Dominion here means:
- treating the property as if you are the **owner**
- using it in a way that **seriously interferes** with the true owner's rights
- depriving the owner of meaningful use or possession

Jerry taking the **car** is different because:
- A car is a major, high-value item
- Tom is fully deprived of it for a meaningful period
- Jerry uses it for his own purposes as if it were his
- Tom cannot access or use his car at all during that time

This is the kind of **serious, substantial interference** that the law calls conversion.

The Shirt vs. Car
Why the shirt is NOT conversion:

- Short duration
- Minimal harm
- Easily returned
- Not a major deprivation
- Not a serious assertion of ownership

Why the car IS conversion:

- Major deprivation
- High-value property
- Long enough to matter
- Jerry uses it as if he owns it
- Tom loses meaningful use of his property

Remember:

Conversion = interference so serious that the law treats it as if the defendant bought the item.
Trespass to chattels = interference that annoys or inconveniences the owner but doesn't rise to that level.

A Helpful Analogy
If someone takes your **pen** for a minute and gives it back → trespass to chattels. If someone takes your **laptop** for the afternoon to write their paper → conversion.
Both involve "control," but only one is **serious enough** to justify forcing the defendant to pay the full value of the item.

If property is **taken, destroyed, sold, kept, or seriously altered,** think conversion. If it's **borrowed, moved, or slightly damaged,** think trespass to chattels.

Hypotheticals:

Hypo 1 – The Laptop Hostage

Nina borrows Paul's laptop "for a minute" but has kept it for two weeks going on three as he works on his term paper.

Analysis:

- Serious interference
- Dominion and control
- Full value damages appropriate.
- Result: Conversion

Hypo 2 – The Jacket

The valet mistakenly gives a customer's expensive jacket to someone else, who walks off with it and never returns it.

Analysis:

- Property permanently lost.
- Serious interference.
- Result: Conversion

Hypo 3 – The Altered Artwork

A gallery intern "touches up" a painting without permission, changing its appearance.

Analysis:

- Significant alteration of property
- Result: Conversion

Hypo 4 – The Sold Bicycle

A roommate sells his roommate's bicycle while he is out of town.

Analysis:

- Selling someone else's property = classic conversion

- Result: Conversion

Chapter 17 – Intentional Infliction of Emotional Distress (IIED)

Spicy Mexican Hot Chocolate Cookies + Extreme & Outrageous Conduct

Spicy Mexican Hot Chocolate Cookies

The IIED Cookie – Extreme, Outrageous, and a Little Too Hot to Handle

IIED is the tort of **extreme and outrageous conduct** – behavior so shocking that it goes beyond all bounds of decency. These cookies capture that sensation perfectly; rich chocolate, warm cinnamon, and a surprising kick of cayenne pepper that hits harder than expected. They're delicious... but they don't play.

Ingredients:

- 1 cup of unsalted butter, softened
- 1 cup granulated sugar
- ½ cup brown sugar
- 2 large eggs
- 1 tsp. vanilla extract
- 2 cups all-purpose flour
- ½ cup cocoa powder
- 1 tsp. cinnamon
- ¼ tsp. cayenne pepper powder (adjust to your liking)
- 1 tsp. baking soda
- ½ tsp. salt
- 1 cup chocolate chips

Instructions:

1. Cream butter and sugars until smooth and fluffy.
2. Add eggs and vanilla; mix until glossy.
3. Stir in flour, cocoa powder, cinnamon, cayenne pepper, baking soda, and salt.

4. Fold in chocolate chips.
5. Scoop dough onto a baking sheet.
6. Bake at 350 degrees Fahrenheit for 10-12 minutes until edges are set.
7. Cool completely — the heat intensifies as the cookies rest, just like emotional distress deepens over time.

IIED is a conduct that is **too much** — too extreme, too outrageous, too harmful. These cookies deliver that same unexpected intensity: a burst of heat that goes beyond what a typical chocolate cookie offers. They're bold. They're memorable. They're a perfect metaphor for a tort that requires behavior beyond ordinary rudeness or negligence.

Intentional Infliction of Emotional Distress (IIED) – Extreme Outrageous Conduct Causing Severe Emotional Harm

IIED protects a person's emotional well-being from conduct that is so shocking, so intolerable, that society refuses to allow it.

Elements of IIED:

- **Extreme and Outrageous Conduct**
  -Beyond all bounds of decency
  -Not mere insults, rudeness or bad behavior

- **Intent or Recklessness**
  -Purpose to cause emotional harm, **or**
  -Reckless disregard for the likelihood of causing it

- **Causation**
  -Conduct must cause the distress

- **Severe Emotional Distress**
  -More than trivial upset
  -Often requires physical manifestations or significant disruption of life

Note: If a conduct makes you think, "that's awful," it's probably not enough. If it makes you think, "that's unthinkable," you're in IIED territory.

Hypotheticals:

Hypo 1 – The Exploitative Landlord

A landlord threatens to evict a single mother unless she agrees to "personal favors," knowing she has nowhere else to go.

Analysis:

- Extreme and outrageous.

- Intent or recklessness present.
- Most likely to cause severe distress
- Result: IIED

Hypo 2 – The Cruel Prank

A boss calls an employee into the office as a prank and tells him that he has an hour to clear his desk he has been fired. He collapses in panic.

Analysis:

- Extreme and outrageous prank.
- Intent to cause emotional distress.
- Severe distress shown.
- Result: IIED

Hypo 3 – The Rude Customer

A customer yells at a cashier and calls him names.

Analysis:

- Rudeness and insults are not enough.
- Result: No IIED.

Hypo 4 – The School Bully

A group of students repeatedly harasses a classmate for months, spreading rumors and encouraging others to isolate her. She develops anxiety and stops attending school.

Analysis:

- Repeated, targeted conduct.
- Severe emotional distress.
- Result: IIED.

Defenses

Chapter 18 – Consent

Snickerdoodle + Permission as a Defense

Snickerdoodles

The Consent Cookie — You Agree to the Cinnamon Before you take a Bite

Consent is all about **permission** — the plaintiff agreeing to conduct that would otherwise be wrongful. Snickerdoodles embody that idea perfectly: you choose to roll the dough in cinnamon sugar. You agree to the flavor. Nothing about the cookie is a surprise.

Ingredients:

- 1 cup of unsalted butter, softened
- 1 ½ cups of granulated sugar
- 2 large eggs
- 2 tsps. vanilla extract
- 2 ¾ cups all-purposed flour
- 2 tsps. cream of tartar
- 1 tsp. baking soda
- ½ tsp. salt
- ¼ cup sugar + 2 tsps. cinnamon (for rolling)

Instructions:

1. Cream butter and sugar until fluffy.
2. Add eggs and vanilla; mix well.
3. Stir in flour, cream of tartar, baking soda, and salt until a soft dough forms.
4. Mix cinnamon and sugar in a small bowl.
5. Roll dough into balls and coat generously in cinnamon sugar.
6. Bake at 350 degrees Fahrenheit for 9-11 minutes until puffy and crackled.
7. Cool completely — every bite tastes exactly like what you agreed to, just like consent in tort law.

Consent is about **knowing participation**. Snickerdoodles require an intentional act: rolling the dough in cinnamon sugar. You choose the coating. You invite the flavor. Just like a plaintiff who consents to conduct cannot later claim it was wrongful.

Consent – Permission that Negates Wrongfulness

Consent is a complete defense to many intentional torts. If the plaintiff **agrees** to the defendant's conduct, the conduct is not wrongful.

Types of Consent

1. **Express Consent**
    - Clear, explicit permission
    - Written
    - Verbal
    - Signed waivers
2. **Implied Consent**
    - Permission inferred from conduct or circumstances.
      Examples:
    - Holding out your arm for a vaccination
    - Participating in a sport that has physical contact
    - Extending you hand for a handshake
    - Sitting in a barber's chair
3. **Apparent Consent**
    - What a reasonable person would interpret as permission. Even if the plaintiff didn't subjectively intend to consent, their actions may reasonably appear to grant it.

Limits on Consent

Consent is invalid when:

- Involuntarily given by duress, coercion, or undue influence
- Given by someone without capacity (young children, mentally incapacitated, etc.).
- By Fraud
- Without knowledge – the person must be aware of what they are consenting to and

also, the consequences/outcome of what they are agreeing to.
- Consent is not a defense when the act is illegal.
- Revocation is permitted before the act is completed, as such the consent is terminated.
- Exceeds the scope of permission. If the defendant goes beyond what was permitted, the excess is actionable. Example: Consent to a haircut is not consent to having your head shaved, unless you went in for a bald cut. A regular shape up extended to a cleanly shaved head, is beyond the scope of permission.

Hypotheticals:

Hypo 1 – The Pickup Game
A player injured during a friendly basketball game.

Analysis:

- By playing, the plaintiff impliedly consented to ordinary contact.
- Result: No battery.

Hypo 2 – The Fraudulent Doctor
A doctor tells a patient a procedure is medically necessary when it is not, and the patient consents based on the lie.

Analysis:

- Consent obtained by fraud is invalid.
- Result: Battery.

Hypo 3 – The Hairdresser's Creation
Client goes in for a wash and set; the hairdresser adds a color to cover the grey without the client's permission.

Analysis:

- Consented to wash and set **not** grey coverage as well.
- Exceeds scope
- Result: May be considered, battery.

Hypo 4 – The Party Kiss
A person leans in for a kiss. The other person does not move away and closes their eyes.

Analysis:

- Apparent consent based on conduct.
- Result: No battery.

Chapter 19 – Self Defense

Ginger Snap Cookies + Reasonable Force Doctrine

Ginger Snap Cookies

The Self Defense Cookie — A Sharp Snap used only When Necessary

Self-defense is **responding appropriately** — using just enough force to protect yourself, but never more than necessary.   snaps embody that idea: they're crisp, sharp, and deliver a spicy snap... but only when you choose to bite. They don't attack first. They respond.

Ingredients:

- ¾ cup of unsalted butter, softened
- 1 cup of granulated sugar
- 1 large egg
- ¼ cup molasses
- 2 cups of all-purposed flour
- 2 tsps. ground ginger
- 1 tsp. cinnamon
- ¼ tsp. cloves
- 2 tsps. baking soda
- ½ tsp. salt
- Extra sugar for rolling

Instructions:

1. Cream butter and sugar until fluffy.
2. Add egg and molasses, mix well.
3. Stir in flour, ginger, cinnamon, cloves, baking soda, and salt unit a soft dough forms.
4. Roll dough into balls and coat in sugar
5. Bake at 350 degrees Fahrenheit for 10-12 minutes until crackled and crisp.

6. Cool completely — the cookie snaps only when pressure is applied, just like self-defense triggered only when force is necessary.

Self-defense is about **measured response**. Ginger snaps are crisp and bold, but only when provoked — you have to apply pressure to get the snap. They don't crumble on their own. They don't overreact. They respond proportionally, just like the doctrine requires.

Self Defense – Reasonable Force to Prevent Imminent Harm

Self-defense allows a person to use **reasonable force** to protect themselves from imminent harmful or offensive contact.

Elements

- **Reasonable belief:** The defendant must reasonably believe they are about to suffer harm.
- **Imminence:** The threat must be immediate — not future or hypothetical.
- **Proportional Force:** The defendant may use only the amount of force reasonably necessary to prevent the harm.

Duty to Retreat (Jurisdiction Specific)

Some jurisdictions require retreat (if safe) before using deadly force. Other jurisdictions follow "stand your ground" rules.

Defense of Others

A person may defend another if they reasonably believe the other person is in danger.

Analysis:

- Was the threat imminent
- Was the belief reasonable
- Was the force proportional

If all three are satisfied, self-defense applies.

Hypotheticals:

Hypo 1 – The Raised Fist

Joseph raises his fist and approaches Michelle as if to strike her. She pushes him away.

Analysis:

- Imminent threat

- Reasonable belief
- Proportional force
- Result: Self-defense

Hypo 2 – The Overreaction
A woman lightly pokes her coworker during a joke. The coworker responds by punching her.

Analysis:

- Force used was disproportionate to the threat.
- Result: No self-defense

Hypo 3 – The Future Threat
Vickie says to Mary, "The next time I see you, I am going to slap you," but makes no movement.

Analysis:

- No imminent threat.
- Result: No self-defense

Hypo 4 – The Defense of Others
A man sees a strange being attacked and pulls the attacker away, using reasonable force.

Analysis:

- Reasonable belief the stranger was in danger.
- Proportional force.
- Result: Defense of others applies.

Chapter 20 – Defense of Property

Shortbread Bars with a Firm Crust + Non-Deadly Force to Protect Land and Chattels

Shortbread Bars with a Firm Crust

The Property Defense Cookie — Firm Enough to Hold Its Shape, Never Excessive

Defense of property is about **protecting what's yours**, but only with **reasonable, nondeadly force**. Shortbread bars capture that balance perfectly: they have a **firm, protective crust** that holds everything together, but they're never harsh or overwhelming. They defend their structure — but gently.

Ingredients:

- 1 cup of unsalted butter, softened
- ½ cup of granulated sugar
- 2 cups of all-purpose flour
- ½ tsp. salt
- Optional: melted chocolate for drizzling

Instructions:

1. Cream butter and sugar until smooth.
2. Add flour and salt; mix until a soft dough forms.
3. Press dough firmly into an 8x8 pan — this creates the "protective crust."
4. Bake at 325 degrees Fahrenheit for 25-30 minutes until edges are lightly golden.
5. Cool completely before slicing into bars.
6. Optional: drizzle with chocolate for a decorative finish.
7. These bars hold their shape without being aggressive — just like the doctrine of defense of property.

Defense of property allows firmness, not aggression. Shortbread bars are sturdy and protective, but never violent.

They mirror the rule perfectly: **you can defend your property — but only with reasonable, nondeadly force.**

Defense of Property – Reasonably, Nondeadly Force to Prevent Intrusion or Interference

Defense of property allows a person to use **reasonable force** to prevent or stop interference with land or personal property.

Key Rule

You may use **nondeadly force** to protect property. You may **never** use deadly force solely to protect property.

Elements

- **Reasonable belief** that property is being invaded or interfered with
- **Reasonable, nondeadly force** used to stop the interference
- **Force must be proportional** to the threat
- **Deadly force is never allowed** unless there is also a threat to personal safety

Defense of Land vs. Defense of Chattels

Defense of Land

- You may use reasonable force to prevent or end a trespass.
- You may not set traps or spring guns.
- You must ask the trespasser to leave if safe to do so.

Defense of Chattels

- You may use reasonable force to recover or protect personal property.
- If property is taken, you must first request it's safe return (if safe to do so).
- Fresh pursuit allows reasonable force to recapture chattels.

Note: If the defendant uses **deadly force** to protect **only property**, the defense fails immediately.

Hypotheticals

Hypo 1 – The Garden Trespasser

A neighbor repeatedly walks across Sam's garden. Sam steps outside and blocks the path, telling the neighbor to leave.

Analysis:

- Reasonable, nondeadly force
- Proportional
- Result" Defense of property applies.

Hypo 2 – The Baseball Through the Window

A child accidently throws a ball through a window. The homeowner grabs the child and shakes him.

Analysis:

- Excessive force
- Property damage does not justify physical aggression.
- Result: No defense.

Hypo 3 – The Purse Snatcher

A thief grabs a woman's purse and runs. She immediately chases him and pull the purse back.

Analysis:

- Fresh pursuit.
- Reasonable force to recapture chattel.
- Result: Defense of property applies.

Hypo 4 – The Booby Trapped Shed

A homeowner rigs a shotgun to fire when the shed door opens. A teenager opens the door and is injured.

Analysis:

- Deadly force used to protect property.

- Traps are never allowed.
- Results: No defense.

Chapter 21

Necessity

Trail Mix Cookies + Public vs. Private Necessity

Trail Mix cookies

The Necessity Cookie — When you use what you Must to Prevent a Bigger Problem

Necessity is all about **choosing the lesser harm** — using or interfering with someone else's property to prevent a greater danger. Trail mix cookies embody the idea: they're made from whatever you have on hand — nuts, chocolate, dried fruit — a practical, resourceful cookie built for emergencies, hikes, storms, and moments when you need something now.

Ingredients:

- 1 cup of unsalted butter, softened
- 1 cup of brown sugar
- ½ cup granulated sugar
- 2 large eggs
- 2 tsps. vanilla extract
- 2 ½ cups of all-purpose flour
- 1 tsp. baking soda
- ½ tsp. salt
- 1 cup chocolate chips
- 1 cup mixed nuts
- 1 cup dried fruit (raisins, cranberries, cherries, etc.)

Instructions:

1. Cream butter and sugars until fluffy.
2. Add eggs and vanilla; mix well.
3. Stir in flour, baking soda, and salt until thick dough forms.

4. Fold in chocolate chips, nuts, and dried fruit — whatever you have available.
5. Scoop onto a baking sheet.
6. Bake at 350 degrees Fahrenheit for 10-12 minutes until edges are golden.
7. Cool completely — these cookies are built for resilience, just like the doctrine of necessity.

Necessity is about **using what you must** to prevent a greater harm. Trail mix cookies are the same; flexible, practical, and built from whatever ingredients are necessary in the moment. They're the "emergency cookie" — the perfect metaphor for a doctrine that allows temporary interference with property to avoid disaster.

Necessity – A Privilege to Interfere with Property to Prevent Greater Harm

Necessity allows a person to interfere with another's property rights when doing so is required to prevent a greater danger.

There are two types:
Public Necessity
Private Necessity
They operate differently — especially when it comes to damages.

Public Necessity:
Complete Defense — No Liability for Damages
Public necessity applies when the defendant acts to protect the **public at large** from a serious threat.

Examples:

- Destroying property to stop a spreading fire
- Breaking into a warehouse to save a wounded employee
- Blocking roads to prevent a chemical spill from spreading

Key Rule
If the action is reasonably necessary to protect the community, the defendant is **not liable** for property damage.

Private Necessity:
Qualified Defense — Privilege to Act, But Must Pay for Damages
Private necessity applies when the defendant acts to protect **their own person or property**, not the public.

Examples:

- Mooring a boat to a private dock during a storm
- Entering someone's land to escape danger
- Breaking a window to avoid drowning or freezing

Key Rule
The defendant may interfere with property but must **pay for any actual damage** caused.
Private necessity = partial defense. Privilege to act, but liability for damage.

Ask yourself in an analysis:
- Was the threat serious?
- Was the action reasonably necessary?
- Was the threat to the public or to the defendant personally?

The answers will decide if it is a **public or private necessity that determines whether it is a complete or qualified defense.**

Hypotheticals

Hypo 1 – The Spreading Fire (Public Necessity)
Firefighters destroy a homeowner's shed to create a firebreak and stop a wildfire from reaching the town.

Analysis:

- Protecting the public.
- Reasonably necessary.
- Result: Complete defense — no liability.

Hypo 2 – The Unexpected Storm (Private Necessity)
A family out jogging an unexpected storm caught them out, they huddled under the porch of a stranger's house.

Analysis:

- Privilege to act.
- Must pay for any damages.
- Result: Qualified defense.

Hypo 3 – The Escaping Hiker (Private Necessity)

A hiker flees a coyote and climbs over a fence onto private land, breaking a few boards.

Analysis:

- Privileged entry to avoid harm.
- Must pay for damages.
- Result: Private Necessity

Hypo 4 – The Chemical Spill (Public Necessity)
City workers bulldoze a fence to access a yard and contain a hazardous spill.

Analysis:

- Protecting the public.
- Reasonably necessary.
- Result: Complete defense

Doctrines Extending Liability

Chapter 22 – Vicarious Liability

Double Chocolate "Employer-Employee" Cookies + Respondeat Superior

The Vicarious Liability Cookie — Two Parts Working Together as One

Vicarious liability is all about **relationships** — one party being held responsible for the actions of another. These double chocolate cookies capture that beautifully: two chocolate, two textures, two components working together to create one unified cookie.
Just like an employer and employee in the scope of employment.

Ingredients:

- 1 cup unsalted butter, softened
- 1 cup of granulated sugar
- ½ cup brown sugar
- 2 large eggs
- 2 tsps. vanilla extract
- 2 cups of all-purpose flour
- ½ cup cocoa powder
- 1 tsp. baking soda
- ½ tsp. slat
- 1 cup chocolate chips
- 1 cup chocolate chunks

Instructions:

1. Cream butter and sugars until fluffy.
2. Add eggs and vanilla; mix well.
3. Stir in flour, cocoa powder, baking soda, and salt until a thick dough forms.
4. Fold in chocolate chips and chocolate chunks — the "two actors" working together.
5. Scoop onto a baking sheet.

6. Bake at 350 degrees Fahrenheit for 10-12 minutes until edges are set.
7. Cool completely — the two chocolates blend into one cohesive cookie, just like vicarious liability blends two actors into one legal responsibility.

Vicarious liability is about **shared responsibility** — one party acting, another party paying. These cookies visually texturally show that duality: two chocolates, one cookie. Two actors, one liability.

Vicarious Liability

Holding One Party Liable for the Tort of Another

Vicarious liability allows a plaintiff to hold a defendant liable for someone else's tortious conduct because of the **relationship** between them.

The most common form is **respondeat superior: An employer is liable for the torts committed by an employee acting in the scope of employment.**

Respondeat Superior: Employer Liability for Employee Torts

Elements:

- **Employee** not an independent contractor.
- **Acting within the scope of employment** (doing the kind of work they were hired to do, during work hours, at a workplace or in an authorized location. Motivate, at least in part, to serve the employer).

Employers are **not** liable for intentional torts unless:

- The jobs involve force (e.g., bouncer, security guards, etc.)
- The tort arises from job related friction
- The employer benefits from the conduct

Frolic v. Detour

- **Detour** (minor deviation) = employer liable (e.g., driver stops to get a bottle of water on the route to make a delivery.)
- **Frolic** (major personal departure) = employer not liable (e.g., on the route to deliver furniture to a customer, the driver stops for a pick-up-game of basketball with his friends; stops by the house to pick up his dog to take to the groomers)

Independent Contractors

General Rule: No Vicarious Liability

Employers are **not** liable for torts committed by independent contractors.

Exceptions:

- Inherently dangerous activities
- Nondelegable duties
- Negligent hiring or supervision

Other vicarious liability relationships:

Partnership: each partner liable for torts committed in the ordinary course of business.

Parents: generally, not vicariously liable, except by statute.

Automobile owners: some states impose liability for family members' driving .

Joint ventures: shared liability for shared enterprise.

Hypotheticals:

Hypo 1 – The Delivery Driver

A delivery driver hits a pedestrian while making deliveries on his assigned route.

Analysis:

- Employee
- Within the scope of employment
- Result: Employer liable.

Hypo 2 – The Personal Errand (Frolic)

A store clerk leaves work to visit a friend across town and hits a cyclist on the way.

Analysis:

- Major personal deviation = frolic
- Result: Employer is not liable.

Hypo 3 – The Bouncer's Punch

A nightclub bouncer punches a patron while removing them from the club.

Analysis:

- Job involves force
- Intentional tort foreseeable
- Result: Employer is liable

Hypo 4 – The Independent Contractor

(1) A homeowner hires a roofer (independent contractor). The roofer negligently drops tools on a passerby.

Analysis:

- Independent Contractor
- No exception applies here
- Result: Homeowner not liable

(2) A large grocery store hires a snow plowing company after a winter storm to clear ice and snow from the parking lot. But they do a poor job, and patches of ice are left and snow. A customer slips and falls.

Analysis:

- Independent Contractor

- Non-delegable duty to keep premises safe for customers (businesses must keep the premises safe for invitees)
- Result: Employer (the store) is liable

Chapter 23 – Strict Liability

Volcano Cookies + Abnormally Dangerous Activities

Volcano Cookies

The Strict Liability Cookie — When the Eruption is Inevitable

Strict liability is about **liability without fault** — when the activity is so inherently dangerous that even the utmost care cannot eliminate the risk. Volcano cookies embody that idea perfectly: they puff, crack and erupt molten chocolate from the center no mater how carefully you bake them. The eruption is built in. Unavoidable. Expected.

Ingredients:

- 1 cup unsalted butter, softened
- 1 cup brown sugar
- ½ cup granulated sugar
- 2 large eggs
- 2 tsps. vanilla extract
- 2 ½ cups all-purpose flour
- 1 tsp. baking soda
- ½ tsp. salt
- ½ cup cocoa powder
- 1 cup chocolate chunks
- Optional: mini marshmallows for "lava"

Instructions:

1. Cream butter and sugars until fluffy.
2. Add eggs and vanilla; mix well.
3. Stir in flour, baking soda, salt, and cocoa powder.
4. Fold in chocolate chunks (and marshmallows if using).
5. Scoop dough into tall mounds on a baking sheet.
6. Bake at 350 degrees Fahrenheit for 10-12 minutes until the tops crack and molten chocolate erupts.

7. Cool slightly — the eruption is part of the cookie's nature, just like strict liability attaches to activities whose risks can't be controlled.

This cookie fits because strict liability applies when the **danger is baked in** — when the activity carries unavoidable risks even with perfect care. Volcano cookies erupt no matter what you do. The risk is inherent. That's strict liability.

Strict Liability – Liability Without Fault for Abnormally Dangerous Activities

Strict liability holds a defendant liable **even if they exercised the utmost care.** The focus is on the **nature of the activity,** not the defendant's conduct.

Abnormally Dangerous Activities

Courts consider several factors (Restatement Approach):

- **High degree of risk**
- **Likelihood of severe harm**
- **Risk cannot be eliminated with reasonable care**
- **Activity not common in the community**
- **Inappropriateness of the activity in the place**
- **Value to the community vs. danger to the community**

If these factors point toward inherent danger, strict liability applies.

Classic Examples:

- Blasting
- Demolition
- Storing explosives
- Crop dusting
- Keeping wild animals
- Hazardous chemical transport
- Largescale firework displays

Animals and Strict Liability

Wild Animals

Owners are strictly liable for harm caused by wild animals, regardless of precautions.

Domestic Animals

Strict liability applies if:

- The owner knows or should know of the animal's dangerous propensities ("one bite rule" for dogs)

Products Liability (Strict Liability in Tort)

Manufacturers and sellers may be strictly liable for defective products that are:

- **Manufacturing defects**
- **Design Defects**
- **Failure to warn**

If the activity is inherently dangerous, uncommon, and cannot be made safe, strict liability is your first line of analysis. Care does not matter.

Hypotheticals:

Hypo 1- The Blasting Company

A construction company uses explosives to clear rocks. Flying debris injured a pedestrian.

Analysis:

- Blasting = abnormally dangerous.
- Precautions irrelevant.
- Result: Strict Liability

Hypo 2 – The Escaped Tiger

A circus tiger escapes and injures a passerby.

Analysis:

- Wild animals = strict liability.
- Result: Strict Liability

Hypo 3 – The Dog with a History

A dog previously bit someone. The owner fails to warn a visitor, and the dog bites again.

Analysis:

- Known dangerous propensity.
- Result: Strict Liability.

Hypo 4 – The Chemical Spill

A company transporting industrial acid overturns a truck, causing burns to nearby drivers.

Analysis:

- Transporting hazardous chemicals = abnormally dangerous.
- Result: Strict Liability.

Closing Note

Take the Recipes With You

You've reached the end of *The Tort Bakery* — but this isn't where tort law ends for you.

This book was never meant to replace your casebook or your outline. It was meant to give you something else: **instinct**. The ability to look at a fact pattern and feel when something is missing. To know when liability collapses because an element never set. To recognize when a defense changes the entire texture of a claim. When you walk into an exam, you won't be carrying recipes.

- You'll be carrying recognition.
- You'll know that negligence needs every ingredient.
- You'll feel when conduct crosses from warm to overdone.
- You'll see when a chain of causation holds — and when it breaks.

That is the goal of this book:

- Not to make the law easier — but to make it **stick**.

If this book helped you understand torts differently, share it with someone else who's still struggling. And if you're reading this on Amazon, leaving a review helps other students find their way into this kitchen too.

The oven is off.
The cookies are cooling.
And you're ready to serve.

Author's Note

Law in Pieces began with memory.

I earned my first law degree with honours through the University of London's External Programme — a path where I was both the teacher and the student. I taught myself the law. There were no daily lectures, no built-in structure, no professor to reassure me that I belonged. There was only discipline, persistence, and the quiet resolve to keep going even when the material felt distant and unforgiving. Years later, I went on to earn my Master of Laws from an ABA-approved law school. By then, I had crossed jurisdictions, crossed borders, and crossed life stages. I was a mother. I had young children. I had studied law once, long ago, and returned to it again in a new country, under a new system, with new expectations.

I remember struggling in a class and asking a question — only to be told, *"Oh, you're a foreign student. That makes sense that you don't understand this.* "In that moment, the issue was no longer doctrine. It was belonging. That experience stayed with me.

- I know what it feels like to teach yourself law.
- I know what it feels like to move between legal systems.
- I know what it feels like to return to study after years away, carrying responsibility, doubt, and the quiet fear of wondering whether you still belong in the room.

Law in Pieces was born from that lived experience. This series is for those who are teaching themselves the law. For those who have studied in one jurisdiction and find themselves learning in another. For those who learn best through narrative, analogy, and connection rather than cold abstraction. For those who have ever felt isolated, incompetent, or tempted to second-guess their journey. These books are not shortcuts. They are bridges. They are designed to make doctrine human — to show how the law fits into real life, real harm, real relationships, and real choices. Each volume breaks complex rules into recognizable patterns, intuitive structures, and stories that stay with you long after the page is turned.

I do not believe the law is meant to be exclusionary. I do not believe confusion is a measure of intelligence. And I do not believe that struggling means you do not belong.
Law in Pieces exists to say: **you do belong**. Wherever you are studying from. However you arrived here. Whatever your path has looked like. These books are for you.

Warmly,
Anjanette G. Seymour, LL.M., LL.B. (Hons.)

www.ingramcontent.com/pod-product-compliance
Lightning Source LLC
LaVergne TN
LVHW022102200926
848481LV00003B/1041